AF488206

AMUSE-BOUCHE

A TASTE OF MELANCHOLY

DANA HUNEKE-STONE

Table of Contents

To my good friend Steven Christofor,
for persistently stoking the fire
and refusing to let the cauldron grow cold.

Free Range

A woman of a certain age,
once a hummingbird in a cage.
Tender places where I've grown.
Wings were clipped.
Still, I've flown.

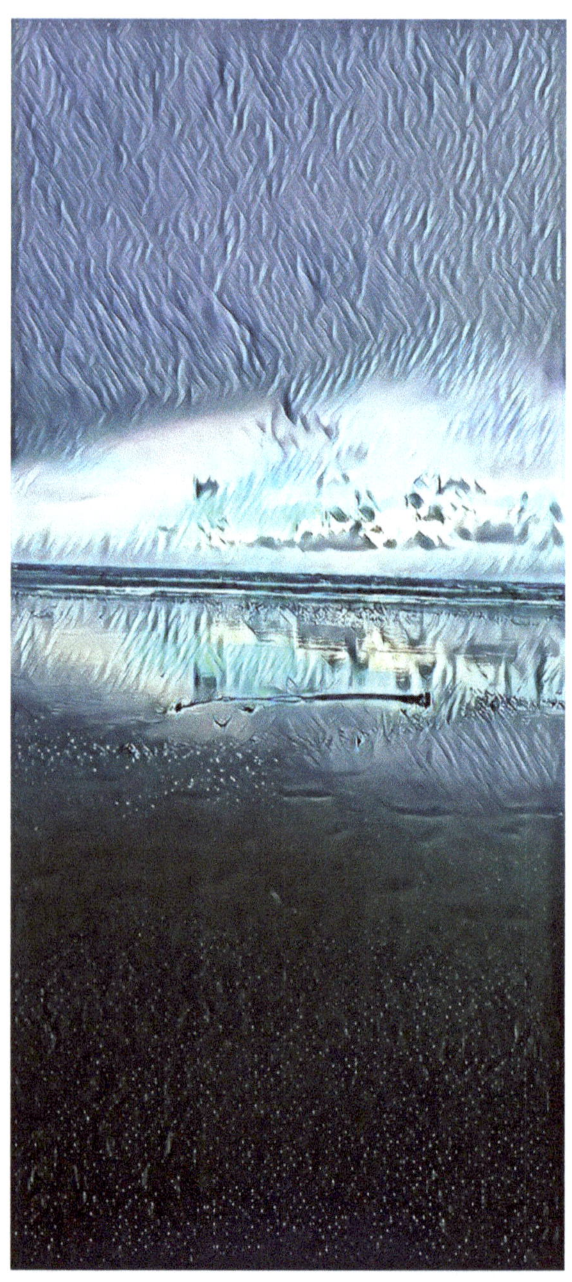

In Between Hue

This emotion not grey,
just a blue that got away.

Sacrificial Kindness

The eternal love of the moon for the sun,
her story begins only once his is done.
The nightly seduction a lesson in grace.
She loves him not ever seeing his face.

Meeting Halfway

Equinox.
Of equal light.
The setting moon puts up a fight.
Submit to sunrise yet, still shine through.
Stormy spring.
More grey than blue.

Orbit

I still love you.
I'm still here. Just,
smaller.
Inside winter, walls
close in on themselves.
Solitude looms,
largest on the horizon.
Behind the sun,
your face.

℞

Who will write the poem of you?
What is the word
that soothes like blue?

Eyeshadow

The frosted lids of morning.
Shades of pink and blue.
Belie the bleak of winter's gaze,
hidden in their hue.

Pacific Kiss

A late bloomer, it took time for me to open my mouth.
The Atlantic is still salty about it.

Walking Papers

Further, each day.
Anointed with spray.
Holy water.
Wayward daughter.
For sky. For stones.
For strength in my bones.
Salted air.
Walking is prayer.

Greening

A sprinkling of stars,
behind curtains of leaves.
At first morning light,
give thanks to the trees.

Netted

A restless sleep.
Insistent moon,
kept watchful eye,
outside my room.
A mind awake,
with trouble fraught.
A dreamless sleep,
in moonbeams caught.

Thin Air

This poem for you not easily wrought.
Words turned wings not easily caught.
A moment here, a season there.
Words like love have souls of air.

Spectral

This moon we call blue,
just ghosts we once knew.
Illumed against night,
disguised as soft light.
Within the waking, the dream.
We see. We are seen.

Gather No Moss

It should be natural as breathing.
Things, and their leaving.
Once loved, now not found.
Inhale. Exhale.
We're circular. We're round.

Pleased To Meet Me

I am the smell of coffee brewing on a rainy Saturday.
I am smoky, inappropriate laughter.
I am the thing you wish you hadn't done.
I'm your favorite.
I'm the one.

DIY

Reassembled bones and scars.
Raven feathers twined with stars.
Wordless. White. Blank pages turn.
She, the pyre on which they burn.
Glowing. In the unknowing.

Search Party

I can't find my words.
I've searched the usual places.
The riverbank. The shoreline. The wild, lonely spaces.
Lifting stones. Unearthing bones.
Skeletons of forgotten poems.

Oyster

Unstrung for you.
Solitary.
Saltwater.
Nascent hue.

Non-Filter

Like smoke I inhaled you.
Tasting your breath.
Traces of sweetness,
mingling with death.
Love is eternal,
leaving remains.
Inhaled like smoke.
Now, ash in my veins.

On The Spectrum

What color is this song?
It's a fistful of violet.
Tar and mud on your shoes.
An explosion of indigo.
The get the fuck out of here blues.

Fermented

What is there left of the fruit on the vine?
Grapes that taste bitter,
now you're no longer mine.

Basic Math

There is no reckoning.
No span of time to reconcile.
No chasm to be crossed.
The geometry is simple.
A piece is missing.
Not lost.

Dialect

I called it love. You called it cage.
I called it passion. You called it rage.
I called it empathy. You called it weak.
I called it feminine. You called it meek.
I called it garden. You called it weed.
I called it devotion. You called it need.
I called it ocean. You called it sky.
I called it eternal. You called it goodbye.

Call Me e.e.

Before the blue, awake.
Sleeping stars of dreams, I rake.
Across the coals of faded flame,
Before the blue, I speak your name.

Runneth Over

Forgiveness is an acquired taste.
Bittersweet on the tongue.
Best when served in gratitude.
By conceding, you have won.

Watercolor

Desire is passive.
We surrender to dreams.
Painted with water,
hearts bleed through at the seams.
Denial is active.
Shadow obscures,
what we mean to forget.
Still,
the wound blurs.

Moving Day

Wondering if winter, like me,
takes routine stock of their possessions (one broken fence post,
two uprooted trees, a mitten)
and pares down,
easing departure.

Mouthwash

Woke with sunshine in my mouth.
Now, I have cloud breath.

Hide And Seek

Today I was called
to the edge of the sea,
under wakening skies.
Searching for thee.
In the crest of the wave,
in the tang of the spray.
The salt in the air,
gave you away.

Opening Remarks

Sunrise.
The innocent hour.
Gently wakes the sky.
Misted river. Liquid cloud.
Before the grace of Time go I.

Jekyll And Hyde

Morning rain,
Sunshine afternoon.
Autumnal hymn.
A wordless tune.

Girdle

Today had no edges.
No spike of sunrise,
shapeless midday.
Summer is muted.
All shades of grey.

Traveling Companion

In case of sun,
you keep a packed bag.
Essentials only.
Pen. Paper. Your mother's ashes.

Ancestors

Skirt hems filled with prayers and stone.
Feathered secrets, root and bone.
A mason jar of sacred water.
Just another moonshiner's daughter.

Hematoma

The natural light of mourning,
a bruise of muted blues.
Hydrangea and wisteria.
The sky is your tattoo.

Meditation

I took a walk.
No talk and a thousand voices heard.
Each shade of grey a blue without a word.

Morning Lonely

Waking on Saturday.
Hours ahead mine alone.
Absence no flesh wound,
it exposes the bone.
The marrow of memory,
rich with regret.
The love we remember.
The pain we forget.

Sweet Surrender

Oh, summer!
It's come to this,
your rosy blush meets autumn's kiss.
Upon your cheek, her cool, dry, breath.
With grace surrender,
a natural death.

Smolder

The smoky haze of distant fires
obscures the truth of lovers and liars.
No depth. No clarity of sky.
We never even said goodbye.

Aphasia

Your poem has no words this year.
An open door delights the wind.
Chimes in ecstatic dance.
Curtains in billowing sail.
This poem is muscle memory and the smell of moss.
It is the mouth of a river.
It has no words.

Declaration

Unapologetically melancholy.
Unspeakably true.
Unashamedly naked. It's me.
It's not you.

All Inclusive

At once in four directions.
Fire, water, earth and air.
An elemental maelstrom.
I find you everywhere.

Xanax

Too much sunshine makes me anxious.
The sky an urgent blue.
I much prefer a languid grey,
its melancholy hue.

Blue Fire. Red Lies.

Red lies. All swagger and pose.
Fleeting bravado, just look at the rose.
Love is blue. Eternal flame.
A rose still a rose,
but she won't have my name.

Synesthesia

This picture paints without a word,
the softest color you never heard.

To Love Like Me. A List in Progress.

1. Practice saying goodbye.
2. Get dirty.
(My love crawls through too tight spaces to rescue precious.)
3. Give it all upfront.
4. Take deep breaths.
5. Live near the sea.
6. Feel small.
7. Break. Again. And again.
8. Keep going.

SURVIVAL

Telepathy

Yesterday, upon the beach,
a message stone within my reach.
The timing no coincidence,
survival calls for vigilance.
So, I walk. Sea spray and foam.
The salted air becomes a poem.

He Ain't Heavy, He's My Brother

Just before the fade to black,
day carries night upon her back.

Church

Any given Sunday.
Wonder to behold.
Heron accepts the eucharist.
In prayer our hands fold.

Embodied

Loneliness dwells in particular smells.
Salted air.
No one there.

Acknowledgments

Acknowledgements are difficult. The potential for falling short. For leaving out.

Depth of gratitude. Love. Your name.

For failing to drive it home.

Like writing a poem.

Thank you. Thank you. Thank you.

To my mother, Valerie: The OG. As ever when I try to write, words pick feelings to a fight. Thus, I relent. I set them free. You yourself are poetry. Oh, how I miss you.

To Chip and Elise. My siblings. My witnesses. My lifelines. Children who don't get heard, turn to word. My heart is full.

To the members of the Rochdale Cooperative and the people of New Haven, Connecticut circa 1989-1998: For both sheltering and exposing me. Literally. We were the right ones in the right place at the right time. Everyone, I love you.

To Madeline and Steve and The Daily Caffe: For fueling and fostering and providing space for the creative in all of us to safely exist. Great coffee, Fine pastries, and Decent people. What an understatement.

To Meg and Larry: For all those candlelit nights spent listening to Kate Bush, Sylvia Plath and our own uncontrollable cackling. The spell was cast. So mote it be.

To Melissa and Nehalem Bay Winery: For generously keeping me in Pinot Noir and their loving, loyal hearts. "And the moon rose over an open field."

To Denise: For providing constant encouragement, levity, (aka side-splitting laughter) Scrabble marathons, and love. Loy!

To all friends and family who've ever been on the receiving end of a poem, read one, or inspired one: Grateful af

To my book coach, Erin Donley: For responding so enthusiastically to my little book and making me feel larger than life.

And lastly, to the magnificent wilds of the Pacific Northwest: My muse. River. Forest. Sea. Where I became me.